Here Is the Wetland

Madeleine Dunphy

ILLUSTRATED BY **Wayne McLoughlin**

HYPERION BOOKS FOR CHILDREN

NEW YORK

For information address Hyperion Books for Children,
114 Fifth Avenue, New York, New York 10011-5690.
Printed in Singapore.
First published in 1996 by Hyperion Books for Children

1 3 5 7 9 10 8 6 4 2

The artwork for each picture is prepared using watercolor.
This book is set in 15-point Bernhard Modern.

Library of Congress Cataloging-in-Publication Data

Dunphy, Madeleine
Here is the wetland / Madeleine Dunphy ; illustrated by Wayne
McLoughlin — 1st ed.
p.   cm.
Summary: Uses a cumulative approach to describe the wetland
ecology of a freshwater marsh, the most common type of wetland in
North America.
ISBN 0-7868-0164-6 (trade)—ISBN 0-7868-2136-1 (lib. bdg.)
1. Wetland ecology—Juvenile literature. 2. Wetlands—Juvenile
literature. [1. Wetlands. 2. Wetland ecology. 3. Ecology.]
I. McLoughlin, Wayne, ill. II. Title.
QH541.5.M3D86   1996
574.5'26325—dc20   95-37206

For Dale

—M. D.

For my little camping friend, Allison

—W. McL.

Here is the wetland.

Here is the water
both shallow and still
that soaks the soil
of this murky, moist world:
Here is the wetland.

ere are the cattails

that grow in the water

both shallow and still

that soaks the soil

of this murky, moist world:

Here is the wetland.

Here is the muskrat

that eats the cattails

that grow in the water

both shallow and still

that soaks the soil

of this murky, moist world:

Here is the wetland.

Here is the mink
who hunts the muskrat
that eats the cattails
that grow in the water
both shallow and still
that soaks the soil
of this murky, moist world:
Here is the wetland.

Here are the bass
that swim from the mink
who hunts the muskrat
that eats the cattails
that grow in the water
both shallow and still
that soaks the soil
of this murky, moist world:
Here is the wetland.

*H*ere is the heron
which stalks the bass
that swim from the mink
who hunts the muskrat
that eats the cattails
that grow in the water
both shallow and still
that soaks the soil
of this murky, moist world:
Here is the wetland.

Here is the frog
that leaps from the heron
which stalks the bass
that swim from the mink
who hunts the muskrat
that eats the cattails
that grow in the water
both shallow and still
that soaks the soil
of this murky, moist world:
Here is the wetland.

*H*ere is the snake

who preys on the frog

that leaps from the heron

which stalks the bass

that swim from the mink

who hunts the muskrat

that eats the cattails

that grow in the water

both shallow and still

that soaks the soil

of this murky, moist world:

Here is the wetland.

Here are the blackbirds

that wing past the snake

who preys on the frog

that leaps from the heron

which stalks the bass

that swim from the mink

who hunts the muskrat

that eats the cattails

that grow in the water

both shallow and still

that soaks the soil

of this murky, moist world:

Here is the wetland.

Here are the bulrushes
that hold up the blackbird
that wing past the snake
who preys on the frog
that leaps from the heron
which stalks the bass
that swim from the mink
who hunts the muskrat
that eats the cattails
that grow in the water
both shallow and still
that soaks the soil
of this murky, moist world:
Here is the wetland.

Here are the coots
that hide in the bulrushes
that hold up the blackbirds
that wing past the snake
who preys on the frog
that leaps from the heron
which stalks the bass
that swim from the mink
who hunts the muskrat
that eats the cattails
that grow in the water
both shallow and still
that soaks the soil
of this murky, moist world:
Here is the wetland.

Here are the ducks

who live near the coots

that hide in the bulrushes

that hold up the blackbirds

that wing past the snake

who preys on the frog

that leaps from the heron

which stalks the bass

that swim from the mink

who hunts the muskrat

that eats the cattails

that grow in the water

both shallow and still

that soaks the soil

of this murky, moist world:

Here is the wetland.

Here is the water

that is home to the ducks

who live near the coots

that hide in the bulrushes

that hold up the blackbirds

that wing past the snake

who prey on the frog

that leaps from the heron

which stalks the bass

that swim from the mink

who hunts the muskrat

that eats the cattails

that grow in the water

both shallow and still

that soaks the soil

of this murky, moist world:

Here is the wetland.

MALLARD

RED-BELLIED WATER SNAKE

MUSKRAT

BULLFROG

MINK

HARDSTEM BULRUSH
(Scirpus acutus)

AMERICAN COOT

GREAT BLUE HERON

SMALLMOUTH
BASS

RED-WINGED
BLACKBIRD

The wetland portrayed in this book is a freshwater marsh. Freshwater marshes are the most common type of wetland in North America. Some other types of wetlands include saltwater marshes, bogs, and swamps. Less than half of the original wetlands in the United States still exist. Wetlands provide habitat for many animals, and more than one-third of the nation's endangered species depend on wetlands for survival.

Like many natural environments, wetlands are threatened by human activities. If you would like to find out ways to help protect wetlands, you can write to:
National Audubon Society, Wetland Educational Materials, Route 4,
Sharon, Connecticut 06069.